KAWSAY

LA LLAMA DE LA SELVA
THE FLAME OF THE JUNGLE

MARÍA VÁZQUEZ VALDEZ

TRANSLATION BY
MARGARET RANDALL

GLOSSARIUM : UNSILENCED TEXTS
the operating system c. 2018

"In order to write her poetry, María Vázquez Valdez has gone beyond herself and arrived at the other shore. The wisdom she has wrought along the way is that of the Great Serpent Sachamama. When we met, she made me think of a hummingbird. Now that I read her, walk beside her, and know her torment, she seems like a drop of light."

—Elena Poniatowska

"Magnificent poetry, at once strong and lyrical; a poetry of mystery, of that which is intuited and can be glimpsed through smoke and the blood canticle. Ancient Shipibo wisdom issuing from an initiation that transmits the universe of a woman of our time, now 'like a disassembled apple / that suddenly shines / and sings.' The ineffable transition from darkness to light in an experience that goes beyond the sensorial; a circle that beats, jungle and mountains; lines that taste like timeless knowledge and word made flesh. This is a hallucinatory book: Here is María Vázquez's Kawsay, The Flame of the Jungle, calling to us from Sachamama, convening us, bewitching us..."

—Chely Lima

"'Poets see with the eyes of angels,' wrote William Carlos Williams, and I have no doubt it is with such eyes that María Vázquez Valdez has expressed all her poetry--especially this new book, Kawsay, the flame of the jungle. All that she has seen and written here comes from the profound internal vision she communicates so brilliantly. I welcome this marvelous new collection to our time."

—José Vicente Anaya

the operating system
GLOSSARIUM : UNSILENCED TEXTS
print//document

KAWSAY: THE FLAME OF THE JUNGLE
(KAWSAY : La Llama de la Selva)

ISBN: 978-1-946031-35-8
Library of Congress Control Number: 2018930541

copyright © 2018 by María Vázquez Valdez
English translation by Margaret Randall
illustrations by Chizuko Osato
edited and designed by Lynne DeSilva-Johnson

For additional questions regarding reproduction, quotation, or to request a pdf for review
contact **operator@theoperatingsystem.org**

*This text was set in Inkbleeda, Minion, Franchise, and OCR-A Standard, printed
and bound by Spencer Printing, in Honesdale, PA, in the USA.
Books from The Operating System are distributed to the trade by SPD/Small Press
Distribution, with ePub and POD via Ingram.*

This text was first published in a first Spanish language edition
by MarEs DeCierto and La Herrata Feliz Editions, Mexico City 2017.

The operating system is a member of the Radical Open Access Collective, a community of
scholar-led, not-for-profit presses, journals and other open access projects. Now consisting
of 40 members, we promote a progressive vision for open publishing in the humanities
and social sciences. Learn more at: http://radicaloa.disruptivemedia.org.uk/about/

Your donation makes our publications, platform and programs possible! We <3 You.
bit.ly/growtheoperatingsystem

the operating system
141 Spencer Street #203
Brooklyn, NY 11205
www.theoperatingsystem.org
operator@theoperatingsystem.org

KAWSAY

LA LLAMA DE LA SELVA
THE FLAME OF THE JUNGLE

A mis abuelas,
en especial a María de Jesús Valdez,
in memoriam.

A todas las almas de la selva.

To my grandmothers,
especially María de Jesús Valdez,
in memoriam.

To all the souls of the jungle.

INDICE / CONTENTS

Porque nada importa,
ni el girasol ni el alcatraz
la pirámide o el árbol

te vas disminuyendo en el viento,
nada importa en el silencio

El hombre viejo habla desde una silla alta,
dice que tus ojos no ven:
todo es "maya" dice *El Vedanta*:
espejismo en movimiento

Nada importa,
ni los años ni el polvo
que amanece en los pulmones

Caída de los dedos en la bruma
buscando sueños

Nada importa porque todo es uno,
todo es uno en este barco,
todo es un sonido,
tú y yo al unísono,
todo es uno

Nada importa entre tú y yo
y un espiral antiguo se desdobla,
te trae hasta mis manos,
agua fresca y pedestal,
cuarzo luminoso en mi vientre
y flores blancas desde el humo

nada importa

Fluye en ríos decapitados
la vida que se esparce y alcanza
las cumbres más límpidas
de águilas y alientos altos

oNE

Because nothing matters,
neither sunflower nor brown bird
pyramid or tree

you grow smaller in the wind,
nothing matters in this silence

The old man speaks from his elevated chair,
he says your eyes do not see:
everything is "maya" *The Vedanta* says:
mirage in movement

Nothing matters,
neither years nor the dust
that dawns in our lungs

Fingers falling through mist
in search of dreams

Nothing matters because all is one,
all is one in this vessel,
all one sound,
you and me in unison,
all is one

Nothing matters between you and me
and an ancient spiral unwinds,
it brings you to my hands,
fresh water and pedestal,
luminous quartz in my womb
and white flowers through the smoke

      nothing matters

Flowing in headless rivers
life scatters and reaches
the purest rivers
of eagles and altitude's breath

desde ahí hasta el fondo del abismo

nada importa,
todo encuentra un sol nuevo,
una luna deslumbrante
o el infierno
                pero nada importa

Nada importa porque todo es uno,
el mismo golpe de tambor
bajo los cielos,
latido hondo que despierta
tras el sueño o la agonía

Éxtasis o angustia
son el mismo potro en celo
tras tu pecho

                Nada importa,

ni tú   ni yo   ni todos

porque todo es uno.

from there to the depths of the abyss

nothing matters,
everything finds a new sun,
a dazzling moon
or hell
        but nothing matters

Nothing matters because all is one,
single drumbeat
beneath the sky,
profound heartbeat that awakens
from dream or agony

Ecstasy or anguish
are the same filly in heat
piercing your breast

        Nothing matters,

Neither you   nor I   nor anyone

because all is one.

I

EL ENCUENTRO

I
THE ENCOUNTER

EPIFANÍA

Crece la claridad
entre la bruma que se disipa,
como un gorrión entre tormentas
que se levanta,
        vela en la marea,
semilla minúscula
que contiene al mundo,
en espera ardiente
y en silencio

Un latido musita sobre los goznes
empolvados de tantos días,
hoguera esperando el fuego

Y un tambor anuncia el regreso,
y el cuerpo vuelve a la sintonía
para que la piel se abra
a la llama que ondea
como un corazón abierto

Vuelve el sol al cuerpo,
fuego líquido que se esparce,
revelación
        limpieza
curación
para dar forma al viento,
dar voz, dar las claves
de los universos escondidos
                dentro
cerraduras hacia el vórtice
del que procede toda forma,
todo signo

Vuelve el sol
para insertarse en su sitio,
magma con voluntad alta,
vuelo de claridad
entre la bruma que se disipa.

As the mist dissipates
it becomes lighter,
a sparrow rising
between storms,
      a sail on the sea surge,
tiny seed
containing the world,
in ardent hope
and silence

A heartbeat whispers on hinges
dusty from so much time,
a hearth awaiting its fire

A drumbeat announces the return,
and the body rejoins harmony
so that skin may embrace
the flame that flutters
like an open heart

Sun returns to the body,
liquid fire that spreads,
revelation
      purity
healing
giving order to the wind,
giving voice, offering keys
to the hidden universes
        within
chains that lead to the vortex
preceding all form,
all sign

The sun comes back
to take its place,
strong-willed magma,
I come back through clarity
through the receding mist.

ENTEÓGENO

Abre un surco en la frente,
fisura que se llenará de todos los colores,
explosión de mundos que se encuentran

Soga que une al mundo de los vivos
con el de los muertos
de noche me quita la cáscara,
sólo quedan unos ojos abiertos,
       vela en medio de un desierto

Pensamientos gangrenados se disuelven
como bruma que se integra a un lago,
y desde la oscuridad comienza a brotar
un verde profundo
desde la selva que me llama,
que se hincha como un corazón
       ardiendo de presencias.

ENTHEOGEN

It opens a furrow in my brow,
a fissure that will fill with every color,
explosion of converging worlds

Rope that ties the world of the living
to that of the dead,
at night I remove the shell,
open eyes are all that remain,
        candle in the middle of a desert

Gangrenous thoughts dissolve
like mist sinking beneath the surface of a lake,
and from darkness a profound green
begins to bloom
from the jungle that calls me,
swelling like a heart
        burning with presences.

SANGRE EN PLENILUNIO

A Ichiro Takahashi

I

Roja miel
burbujea desde otro umbral,
cósmica hiel
que al cruzar la garganta
se vuelve dedos luminosos

Consciente,
vibra por sitios inauditos
en un volcán que crece
hasta alcanzar el grado de implosión
donde toda forma se disloca

La conocí una noche
            en plenilunio,
—el alma postrada invocaba luz—

esa nueva vida se erigió
con la potencia de un huracán,
hinchando de vida
            los puntos yertos,
los ríos inmóviles,
las estrellas marchitas

Barrió con mi memoria,
y como recién nacida
miré todo de nuevo, con
el terror
del que brota al fin
de un abismo en agonía.

II

Roja y espesa,
trajo las tablas de la ley
bordadas de fuego
y de plantas sagradas

BLooD IN THE FULL MooN

I

Red honey
bubbles across another threshold,
cosmic bile
turning to luminous fingers
as it descends my throat

Conscious,
it vibrates in outrageous places
in a volcano that grows
until ready to explode
where all form pulls apart

I met her on a night
        of full moon
—her prostrated soul invoked light—

that new life soared
with a hurricane's power,
filling with energy
        rigid,
immovable rivers,
fading stars

She erased my memory,
and like a newborn
I saw everything anew,
with the terror
that emanates from the depths
of an abyss in agony.

II

Red and dense,
she brought the tablets of the covenant
rimmed in fire
and sacred plants

En ellas refulgía el sino,
la sangre hirviendo
que contiene los misterios
y todas las respuestas

Se apareció
rompiendo las sombras,
unidas entre sí
como un cascarón caduco,
moviéndose entre cantos

      mariri, mariri, mariri

La vi elevarse como una fumarola,
velo que envolvió toda la carne
exprimiendo desde la angustia
el amor,
colapsando el cuerpo en inmensa sístole
        infinita.

III

Mi primer encuentro me
rompió hasta el olvido,
me volvió un Ser despojado
de identidad y de memoria

El dolor era insoportable,
el cuerpo se constreñía
en el tormento del infectado,
mientras esa sangre
limpiaba los canales
        putrefactos,
despertando los jardines en
        cenizas

Traté de cerrar la puerta
        a ese ciclón,

pero su fuerza destruyó mi casa
—lo que creí que era mi casa—
y me arrancó todo
hasta la pérdida absoluta,
hasta el vacío

Destiny shone in them,
boiling blood
containing the mysteries
and all the answers

She appeared
breaking through the shadows,
fused among themselves
like a worn-out shell,
moving between songs

mariri, mariri, mariri

I saw her rise like a funnel of smoke,
a cloak shrouding her flesh
forcing love
from anguish,
her body collapsing
in one immense and infinite
          contraction.

III

My first encounter
put an end to forgetting,
I became a Being dispossessed
of identity and memory

The pain was unbearable,
my body constricted
in the torment of one infected,
while that blood
cleansed putrefied
          channels,
waking gardens
          turned to ash
I tried to close the door
          against that cyclone,

but its power destroyed my house
—what I believed was my house—
and took everything
even absolute loss,
even nothingness

Mi resistencia aumentó el terror
en medio de la amnesia,
en adolorida convulsión
hasta que comprendí
que debía soltar, aceptar
lo que viniera
              —analogía violenta de la vida—,
y entonces todo encontró

su lugar de nuevo,
las piezas de mí   ya limpias
se unieron dulcemente,
y el fuego creció dentro,
incendio aún
pero en ofrenda

El alma
              encendida
respiró profundo al fin,
llenándose de Vía Láctea,
heredera del mundo,
descendiente humilde
              de gigantes,
para elevar un canto

              murmullo perfumado
de todos los principios.

IV

Esa luna llena
su sangre me desbordó,
líquido oscuro
más amargo que los mares

Esa noche la encontré:
Señora de la Floresta,
hermosa y terrible
como la naturaleza
en su devastador portento

Y ahí se quedó palpitando,
haciendo grande
mi hambre de alma

My resistance increased my terror
in the midst of amnesia,
in painful convulsion
until I understood
I must loosen my grip, accept what would come
                —life's violent analogy—,
and then everything found

its place once again,
the pieces of myself   clean now
reassembled sweetly,
and the fire grew within,
still fire
            but one of offering

As it burned
            my soul
breathed deep at last,
filling itself with Milky Way,
inheritor of the world,
humble descendant
            of giants,
to raise a song

            sweet-smelling whisper
of every principle.

IV

That full moon's blood
overflowed in me,
dark liquid
more bitter than the seas

That night I found her:
Lady of the Dell,
beautiful and terrible
like nature itself
in devastating wonder

And she remained there
throbbing,
swelling my hunger for soul

Gran Serpiente
        Sachamama,
sembradora de mundos
en galaxias vacías,
trajo con la violencia desmedida
de lo justo
el horizonte transformado
de caos
        en flor.

Great Serpent
        Sachamama,
Sower of worlds
in empty galaxies,
bringing a horizon
transformed from chaos
into flower
        with the immeasurable
violence of justice.

II

LA SELVA Y LOS ANDES

II

THE JUNGLE AND THE ANDES

SONIDOS

En colores se desenrollan
los sonidos de la selva,
a donde no llega
el latigazo de la electricidad
ni el concreto,
y la médula de las lianas
es una sangre iridiscente

Una voz
envuelta en noche
abre todos los pétalos de
su pelambre,
palpita desde un vientre
oscuro y hondo,
ácido como un origen
sedimentado en luz

Desde todos los confines
los sonidos se vuelcan
en colores que palpitan
en los oídos

Exuberancia que se yergue
en majestuoso derroche
hasta comerlo todo,
consumirlo hasta el tuétano

La selva es un tambor
de grillos traducidos
en luciérnagas, vida
hirviendo en un fogón
que canta y no culmina.

SOUNDS

The sounds of the jungle
unfold as colors,
where neither the scourge
of electricity
or concrete are present,
and the marrow of jungle vines
is iridescent blood

A voice
shrouded in night
displays all the petals
of its pelts,
it beats from the deep
dark womb,
sharp as genesis
rooted in light

From every confine
noises express themselves
in colors palpitating
in our ears

Exuberance rises
in majestic profusion
until it consumes everything
consumes it to the core

The jungle is a drumbeat
of crickets becoming
fireflies, life
bubbling on a bonfire
that crackles endlessly.

TABACO

Una esponja   verde   translúcida
succiona cada poro,
            colibrí
                    ubicuo

Tras la primera noche
en silencio
y sin más luz
que las luciérnagas,
mi cuerpo se abre
            al firmamento

El amanecer en la *maloka*
nos encuentra en invocación
empapados en una flama
que congrega
oraciones blancas

Estamos encendidos
            para abrir
las puertas del cuerpo,

y unos sorbos de tabaco
barren las entrañas
hasta que el mundo
parece de agua,
lleno de sombras
y de luces nuevas

Nos hemos abierto
como un mar
sin orillas
lanzado al cielo,
agua
            ya
                    sin reflejos,
escurriendo   su   memoria
hasta pulir las estrías
de estos palacios de cristal
y sangre.

TOBACCO

A green   translucent   sponge
sucks at every pore
            ubiquitous
                        hummingbird

Through the first night
in silence
and with no light
but the fireflies,
my body opens
            to the firmament

In the *maloka*[1]
dawn finds us in prayer
devoured by a flame
that gathers
white invocations

We are on fire
            so we may open
the body's doors,
and a few sips of tobacco
clear our bowels
until the world
turns to water,
filled with shadows
and new lights

We have opened ourselves
like a shoreless
sea
cast to the sky,
water
            without reflections
                                    now,
draining   its   memory
to polish the striations
of these palaces of cristal
and blood.

---

1   *A round hut where meditation took place.*

Río

Manso arador
        paciente cabalga
para lamer las riberas
        de la chacruna
junto a las lianas
que concentran
los umbrales

De mañana me sumerjo en el río
donde pescan los murciélagos
y se bañan   libélulas
                    bicéfalas

        Agua de luz, agua de estrellas,
        Pachamama viene del cielo

Me recuesto en la corriente
y escucho un himno
para el mundo

        desde un pequeño cuerpo
sumergido
        enamorado.

The tranquil tiller of fields
        moves patiently
so he may lap the chakruna's[2]
        shores
beside the vines
that link
thresholds

In the morning I enter the river
where bats fish
and   two-headed dragonflies
                        bathe

     Water of light, water of stars,
     Pachamama descends from the sky

I rest on the current
and listen to a hymn
for the world

     from a small body
submerged
     in love.

---

2   *Chakruna, or Psychotria viridis, is a perennial shrub of the Rubiaceae family. In the Quechua languages it is called chacruna or chacrona. In Quechua, chaqruy is a verb meaning "to mix".*

DIEZ DÍAS

En un desnudo
cuarto de madera
está lo que ya no tengo

En medio de la selva amazónica
vine a encontrar lo que soy
y a dejar lo que nunca
he tenido

Esta orilla del mundo
no conoce la electricidad,
la luz aquí es real:
llega con el sol
y se va al atardecer

Un silencio exuberante
hierve   de   verdes,
envuelve una médula de carne
que es bañada por el río,
claro como un bocado
de nieve derretida,
cantando ondinas
          de espuma

En esta selva
se alzan las ceibas
absortas en el misterio,
enredando lianas,
describiendo signos,
lanzando su bendecida soga
hacia los muertos
          hacia mí

En este cuarto de madera
una vela humilde me ilumina,
una cama pequeña me arropa
y una hamaca mece al amanecer

Nada más y tanto,
tan sólo y suficiente

TEN DAYS

What I no longer have
resides in a naked
wooden room

I came to the Amazon jungle
to find what I am
and leave
what I never had

This side of the world
does not know electricity,
here light is real:
it comes with the sun
and departs at dusk

An exuberant silence
seethes   in   greens,
wraps around a core of flesh
bathed by the river,
transparent as a mouthful
of melted snow,
singing nymphs
            of foam

Lost in mystery
kapok trees
rise in this jungle,
tangling vines,
describing signs,
tossing their blessed rope
to the dead
            to me

In this wooden room
a modest candle illuminates me,
a small bed holds me
and a hammock sways at dawn

                    Nothing more and so much,
                    only this and enough

Aquí los apegos se desvanecen,
la frugalidad
        —suculenta—
se pone al centro del cuerpo
que durante diez días
no comerá ni usará químicos,
no pronunciará palabras

Un himno
comienza a alzarse humilde
para pedir al Ser
uno de sus destellos,
y lo no ingerido
se suma a lo incorpóreo
y comienza a refulgir

La inmovilidad conjura lo real,
diluye la ilusión,
quiebra los turbios espejos
que esconden
lo que es

Silencio y ayuno llenan los vacíos,
huecos desbordados
de miseria inexistente

Gotas de luz
florecen
en un tibio aroma
        de canto
                y firmamento.

Here attachments fade,
frugality
       —succulent—
installs itself in the center of the body
that for ten days
will not eat or use chemicals,
will not pronounce words

A humble hymn
begins to rise
asking the Being
for a bit of its glow,
and the not ingested
joins the immaterial
and begins to shine

Immobility conjures what is real,
dilutes illusion,
fractures the turbid mirrors
that hide
what is

Silence and fasting fill the empty spaces,
places overflowing
with nonexistent misery

Drops of light
flower
in a warm breath
       of song
              and firmament.

PRIMER ASCENSO:
BRILLO EN LA PENUMBRA

Un murmullo vertido en sombras
parpadea en claves primigenias
para escarbar en la ausencia

He venido apagando días
de tiempo aprisionado
y aliento que alimenta
un engranaje sin sentido

Pero aquí todo tiene
una sabiduría absorta en la vida,
aquí no hay más
que la verdad envuelta en selva,
en la canción interminable del río,
en el ciclo pautado por el sol,
que es brillo y es penumbra

Aquí todo tiene su lugar,
todo tiene su función
que se desliza
como pieza impostergable

He llegado aquí
buscando a esa maestra
que se esconde en lo recóndito,
a consultar su oráculo
de noche y de silencio,
de vida conectada
en sus principios,
ya sembrada   entre mis huesos

He venido aquí
para atisbar al viento
escondido entre mis venas
como a un brujo cauteloso
que en mi centro me sustenta

FIRST ASCENT: BRILLIANCE IN THE SHADOWS

A whisper scattered among shadows
blinks a primitive code
to excavate absence

I have been extinguishing days
imprisoned time
and breath that feeds
a meaningless assemblage

But here everything possesses
a wisdom absorbed with life,
here there is nothing more
than truth wrapped in jungle,
in the endless river song,
in the cycle marked by the sun,
both brilliance and shadow

Here everything is in its place,
everything has its purpose
going where it must
impossible to delay

I have come here
searching for that teacher
who hides in the remote place,
I want to consult her oracle
of silence and night,
of life connected
in its beginnings,
already planted   between my bones

I have come here
to glimpse the wind
hiding in my veins
like a prudent healer
sustaining me from my center

Y todo lo he encontrado
explotando en el viento,
semillas de sol cautivas

Todo lo he encontrado
en una ardiente plenitud
que es cuerpo y es conciencia

Porque en lo profundo todo se mueve,
todo se integra, se despierta,
en lo oscuro todo se enciende y se apaga,
se contiene y también se suelta

Al final el camino empieza,
abre surcos en sí mismo
para florecer respuestas
en tierra nueva

germinando.

And I have found everything
exploding in the wind,
the sun's captive seeds

I have found everything
in the ardent plenty
that is body and conscience

Because everything moves in the depths,
everything integrates, awakens,
in the dark everything lights up and burns out,
contains itself and also moves free

The path begins at the end,
opens furrows in itself
so it may bloom answers
upon new ground

   and take root.

SEGUNDO ASCENSO: FRACTAL.

En caída hacia el cielo
se despliega túnel
que llega hasta lo hondo
de la materia que es carne

Su casa es un fractal
y ella una serpiente
que difumina sus contornos

Está esperando
con respuesta precisa,
lo sabe todo
sin tiempos ni distancias

Pero también responde
a lo no formulado,
sabe de preguntas
que no son dichas

Esta noche he caído
por el túnel más profundo
y al llegar al fondo encuentro
un mar de formas perfectas
y colores brillantes
en la espesura de la noche:
       tejido primitivo

Ella me espera en su casa
       —extensión de ella—
me mira desde un perfil alargado,
ojo que ha cruzado eras

No le tengo miedo,
me siento iluminada
en su reflejo de respuestas

SECOND ASCENT: FRACTAL.

Falling toward sky
a tunnel unfolds
and arrives at the depth
of that matter called flesh

Her house is a fractal
and she is a serpent
who blurs its edges

She waits
with precise response,
she knows everything
devoid of time or distances

But she also answers
what has not been asked,
knows about
silent questions

Tonight I have fallen
into the deepest tunnel
discover a sea
of perfect forms
and brilliant colors at the end:
a primitive weave
        in the density of night

She waits for me in her house
        —extension of herself—
looks at me from her elongated profile,
eye that has crossed time

I am not afraid of her,
I feel illuminated
in her reflection of answers

cirujana psíquica
me sana el cuerpo,
purifica mis entrañas,

levanta en una ofrenda
mi corazón
despeñado en sí mismo.

a psychic surgeon
        she heals my body,
purifies my essence,

raises my heart
in offering
as it implodes.

TERCER ASCENSO: CORAZÓN

El movimiento del cuerpo
ha ido disminuyendo
poco   a   poco

de maremoto
se ha vuelto espuma
que llega a las orillas,
bordes mansos como
lenguas tibias

El pulso a ratos se sobresalta
pero se va volviendo suave
como una pincelada de nube
en el horizonte

Esta noche
      —quinto día en la selva—
la encuentro por tercera vez

Débil,
apenas me pongo de pie
en esta noche azul
y mi corazón decide
que debo mirar
a lo más hondo desde
lo más inmóvil

Casi no puedo respirar
pero entro
por el ojo de la aguja,
y detrás me espera
un espíritu ancestral
en el que se conjugan
los seres de la selva

      aves y líquenes
otorongo y ayaymama

THIRD ASCENT:
HEART

The movement of my body
has slowed
little   by   little

from tidal wave
I have become foam
reaching the shores,
gentle edges
like warm tongues

At times   my pulse startles
but calms itself again
like a brushstroke of cloud
on the horizon

This night
             —my fifth in the jungle—
I find her for the third time

Weak,
I struggle to my feet
on this blue night
and my heart decides
it must look
at the deepest place
from that which is most quiet

Almost unable to breathe
I enter
through the needle's eye,
and an ancestral spirit
awaits me in that place
where the beings of the jungle
come together

        birds and lichen
otorongo and *ayaymama*

en la selva
hasta el silencio suena

Para encontrar
a ese espíritu
debo cruzar el sonido,
debo cruzarme a mí misma
y un palacio de espejos
quebrados por la tormenta

Llego al otro lado,
apenas un hilo de aliento
y entonces la veo
            al centro,
perfecta
con su perfil alargado

Me está esperando
y mi collar de preguntas
se desvanece
en fuego blanco.

in the jungle
until the silence sounds

To find
that spirit
I must cross the barrier of sound,
I must cross myself
and a palace of mirrors
shattered by the storm

Barely a thread of breath
I reach the other side,
and then I see her
       in the center,
perfect
with her elongated profile

She is waiting for me
and my necklace of questions
disappears
in white fire.

CUARTO ASCENSO: FUEGO

De día viene   y tan distinta

Siempre la vi de noche,
ataviada de figuras geométricas,
con su cetro de ébano
para romper la oscuridad

Ahora la veo sonando entre tambores,
palpitando como una cobra
que se alza en una iniciación
prehistórica

Llena de colores
viste mi carne,
empuja mis caderas
a una danza antigua,
levanta mis manos
hasta describir dibujos
de eras geológicas
y fuegos hondos de un volcán,
profundo fuego

desde el centro de la tierra,
fuego en implosión
creando mundos simultáneos,
abriendo rutas
que son surcos,
estrellas rojas en plenitud,
espasmos encendidos
de planetas colosales y
fuego,
        tanto fuego
arrasando
con la memoria
y el olvido,
trayendo una urdimbre
desconocida

FOURTH ASCENT:
FIRE

She comes by day   looking so different

I always saw her at night,
dressed in geometric images,
shattering darkness
with her ebony scepter

Now I see her dreaming among drums,
swaying like a cobra
rising in prehistoric
initiation

She dresses my flesh
in colors
urges my thighs
into an ancient dance,
raises my hands
until they describe
drawings of geological eras
and deep volcanic explosions,
profound fire

from the earth's center,
imploding fire
creating simultaneous worlds,
opening pathways
that are furrows,
dome of red stars,
lightning spasms
of colossal planets
and fire,
            so much fire
laying waste
to memory
and forgetting,
bringing with it
an unknown plan

en eso que era el mundo,
pero que ya no es más

Una puerta dejó entrar
otro lenguaje,
ojos distintos
y colores nuevos,
formas inhumanas
y música que es conjuro
y también salmo
para despertar,
para al fin sacudir
la pobreza de la vida,
los abismos negros,
la ceniza

Todo crujió en esa implosión
pero sin violencia,
una miel ardiente cubrió las formas
sin amargura,
sin veneno,
          para crear vida,
para traer consigo
el rompimiento.

for this that was the world
but is no longer

A door opened to
another language,
different eyes
and new colors,
non-human forms
and music that is incantation
and also psalm
waking me,
at last shaking off
life's poverty,
its dark chasms,
its ashes

Everything groaned in that implosion
but peacefully,
a passionate honey covered it all
without bitterness,
without poison,
        creating life,
and bringing with it
the final rupture.

QUINTO ASCENSO: ROMPIMIENTO

Cinco días de ayuno
y cuatro ascensos:
      el cuerpo se ha vaciado,
la mente se apagó
y el alma brilla suspendida
      en sí misma

Noche cerrada
y la invoco una vez más,
la última en la selva

En la *maloka*
bebo el tuétano de las lianas
y su alquimia con la chacruna
despierta el fuego,
pero esta noche su tardanza
      —inusitada—
me invita a invocarla
una vez más

Espero en el silencio,
en la profunda oscuridad,
hasta que me llama el cielo
afuera

      vuela, vuela, condorcito
      vuela, vuela, aguilita

Y de pronto
un zumbido me traspasa,
el mundo se rompe
más violentamente que nunca,
el cuerpo se retuerce
y apenas alcanzo a volver

      marirí, marirí, marirí...

FIFTH ASCENT: RUPTURE

Five days of abstinence
and four ascents:
            my body has emptied,
my mind is uninhabited
and my soul shines suspended
            within itself

An overcast night
and I call out to it once more,
the last in the jungle

In the *maloka*
I drink the sap of vines
and its alchemy with the chacruna
wakes the fire,
but tonight its delay
            —unusual—
invites me to invoke it
one more time

I wait in silence,
in the depth of darkness,
until the sky outside
beckons

            fly, fly, little condor
            fly, fly, little eagle

And suddenly
a whirring pierces me,
the world shatters
more violently than ever,
my body buckles
and I almost don't come back

mariri, mariri, mariri

Entonces sucede:
un maremoto me arrastra
fuera del mundo
hacia galaxias desconocidas

Una ola desbocada
me lanza a otro universo
en un choque eléctrico
que dura eras

Todo el dolor   descontrolado
me posee
como un jinete sin brida,
y de llevarme a mundos lejanos,
de pronto me lanza
con la misma fuerza
a mi inconsciente

Mi dolor físico es inaudito,
ya no soy yo,
me colapsé como una nave
que choca contra sí misma

Mi reverso, terrible y desnudo
se revela sin códigos,
formas impresionantes,
en amarillo eléctrico,
surcada de espinas negras,
palabras como estiletes,
bisturís haciendo manar   sangre
                                   negra

Ahora el dolor
no sólo es físico,
y con el sistema nervioso
hecho pedazos,
las lágrimas son un consuelo
inalcanzable

Un murmullo trae los significados para mí
incomprensibles,
me arropan
y luego muestran el
otro lado:

Then it happens:
a great wave sweeps me
out of this world
toward unknown galaxies

In an electric shock
lasting eras
a wild surf
heaves me into another universe

All pain   defiant
possesses me
like a rider without reins,
and after taking me to far-off worlds,
suddenly with that same force
throws me back
into my unconscious

I have never known such physical pain,
I am no longer myself,
I am shipwrecked like a vessel
colliding with itself

My other side, naked and terrible,
reveals itself without codes,
impressive forms
in electric yellow,
furrowed with black thorns,
words like stilettos,
scalpels drawing   black
                                blood

Now my pain
exceeds the physical,
and with my nervous system
in pieces,
tears are an impossible
comfort

A murmur brings me impenetrable
meanings,
they dress me
then show me
the other side:

el jardín al que debo navegar

En tus ojos de aguas infinitas
se bañan las estrellitas

Tanto dolor fertiliza,
sacude el pecho de abrojos
hasta que queda   sólo   una vela
ondeando en la tormenta,

iluminando la vida,
sus desaciertos y su sentido,
envolviendo el mundo
con lo único que sobrevive
al vendaval:

un amor inquebrantable,
amor de luna llena,
sedimento humano,
último reducto   del Ser

vestido de terciopelo
de la conciencia

Verse a sí misma es terrible,
enfrentar el fondo sin asideros
es aterrador,
pero tras la imagen
se desdobla lo que es,
ligero y profundo,
despojado de todo
menos de esa flama amorosa
que da todo sentido
y sustento

que levanta de la fosa
a los condenados   como yo

surcados sin embargo
por esa luz inmarcesible.

the garden where I must navigate my ship

In your eyes of endless waters
small stars bathe

Such pain pollinates,
weeds my breast of thistles
until only   a candle   remains
flickering in the storm,

illuminating life,
its errors and meaning,
wrapping the world
with all that survives
the gale:

an unbreakable love,
a full-moon love,
human sediment,
last bastion   of Being

wrapped in the velvet
of consciousness

To glimpse oneself is terrible,
to face the depth alone
terrifying,
but in that image
what is unfolds,
light and profound,
cleansed of everything
but that loving flame
that gives all meaning
and sustenance

let the condemned   like me
rise from the pit

unearthed by this
immeasurable light.

INTERLUDIO

El afuera es un recuerdo
breve

La carne vibra
con otro ritmo

mariří, mariří, mariří

La identidad encuentra
nuevos códigos,
como una manzana
desollada
que de pronto se ilumina
y canta.

INTERLUDE

What lies beyond is
        brief memory

My flesh vibrates
with another rhythm

        mariri, mariri, mariri

My identity finds
new codes,
like a disassembled
        apple
that suddenly shines
and sings.

SEXTO ASCENSO: LOS ANDES

A Tatiana Solana

Lejos de la selva,
en la cúspide de Perú,
la nieve enciende el cielo
como nubes pétreas
sobre la cordillera

       allá
donde habita el cóndor
se alzan majestuosos
                Apus,
guardianes antiguos,
colosos impecables

En lo alto de una montaña
la encuentro una noche,
lejos de su casa tibia y húmeda,
placenta a la que me había
          ceñido

En los Andes
el vuelo es helado,
y mi carne se constriñe

Con el sobresalto
llega una oleada fresca
de invierno permanente
en Luna llena

El resplandor surge
a medianoche
con tanta plata sobre hielo,
bandeja de joyas
que visten el horizonte

Ella me pone de pie una vez más
para acercarme al cielo,

SIXTH ASCENT: THE ANDES

For Tatiana Solana

Far from the rain forest,
at Peru's summit,
snow lights the sky
like rocky clouds
on the mountain ridge

      there
where the condor lives
majestic Apus
          rise,
ancient guardians,
impeccable giants

In the far reaches of a mountain
I find her one night,
far from her moist warm home,
the placenta to which I had been
      clinging

In the Andes
flight is glacial,
and my flesh constricts

With the shock
comes a fresh wave
of permanent winter
in full Moon

Its radiance shines
at midnight
with so much silver on ice,
a sheet of jewels
adorning the horizon

She stands me upright once more
to bring me closer to the sky,

para abrir mi cráneo
en una alabanza
simultánea al canto
del mundo

Afilada perfección,
          señal de brillo metálico,
claridad gélida
y sobrio encuentro
con la suntuosa madrugada

Sobre un pico nevado
la luz afilada brota,
          entraña de un volcán
que condensa los vientos altos,
cúspides de mundos antiguos,
salmos que describen
el origen y el final

He venido tan cerca del cielo
a dejar mi ofrenda,
despacho de flores y semillas,
de amor nacido del abismo

He venido
          para fertilizar la tierra
donde se desvaneció mi tumba.

to open my skull
in simultaneous
praise song
to the world

Perfect profile,
          sign of metallic brilliance,
icy clarity
and somber encounter
with sumptuous dawn

On a snowy peak
harsh light surges,
          entrails of the volcano
that intensify the high winds,
peaks of ancient worlds,
 psalms that describe
the beginning and the end

I have come so close to the sky
 to leave my offering,
scattering of flowers and seeds,
love born of the abyss

I have come
          to fertilize the earth
where my tomb disappeared.

MILAGRO

For Tito La Rosa

Desde el silencio
la nada explota en colores,
y el hilo finísimo de un charango
teje la urdimbre más delicada

Un milagro se eleva
como incienso y cerradura,
enhebra las orillas uniendo los abismos,
 dibuja luciérnagas
en la noche más profunda

Una membrana se extiende,
constelación escrita sin palabras,
edificando otros picos nevados,
hondos como el aire

Ahí los toques primigenios,
horizontes desdoblados,
jaguares antes cautivos,
faros sobre el mar
ya sin tormentas.

MIRACLE

For Tito La Rosa

Out of the silence
a many-colored nothingness explodes,
and the charango's fine thread
weaves its most delicate warp

A miracle rises
like incense and keyhole,
threads the edges
linking fissures,
tracing fireflies
in the profundity of night

A membrane stretches out,
constellation written without words,
creating other snow-capped peaks,
deep as air

There is original touch,
horizons unfolding,
once captive jaguars,
lighthouses overlooking the sea
without storms now.

III

EL RETORNO

III

THE RETURN

COLLAR EN LA DISTANCIA

A mis compañeros en la selva, y para siempre.

La selva abrió sus manos verdes
                            para dejar ir
pero su abrazo penetró en la médula,
como la luz impregna el agua
de brillos inauditos

Las noches trajeron
el silencio más vivo,
y un sueño se quedó
revoloteando como pez
              con alas,
embriagado de sí mismo
y entre ceibas
              para siempre

Tanta miel
construye colosos
                      dentro,
inalterables luciérnagas
en estos cuerpos,
y una voz rondando en la *maloka*

inflama de presencias
la distancia,
regresa al vuelo
invocado,
retumba entre los huesos,
cierne de imágenes
cualquier penumbra

Y este cuerpo
sumiso al alma
              que se eleva
como gota incendiada
por esa savia
—erial iluminado—,
              este cuerpo dócil

NECKLACE IN THE DISTANCE

For my companions of the jungle, now and always.

The jungle opened its green hands
          to release us
but its embrace penetrated our core,
as light impregnates water
with an unprecedented sheen

Night brought
the loudest silence,
and a dream that twisted
and turned like winged
          fish,
drunk on itself
and tangled in seaweed
          forever

So much honey
creates giants
          within,
immutable fireflies
in these bodies,
and a voice sounding through the *maloka*

inflames the distance
with presences,
takes flight again
when invoked,
resounds among bones,
sifting images
from any shadow

And this body
dependent upon the dawn
          that rises
like a drop of water
on fire in that sap
—illuminated wasteland—,
          this docile body

se vuelve el río
        de Rinquía,
caudal que a ratos se desborda,
invisible y en silencio

Un ramillete dejó ir la selva,
mapa de hilos enhebrados
como venas que unen sangre,
formas que emergen
poco a poco,
entre cantos y caminos,
collar de flores

en el cuello de una diosa
palpitando en la distancia,
        tan profundo.

returns to
      the Rinquía River,
now and then flooding its shores,
invisible and silent

The jungle lets go of a branch,
a map of tangled threads
like veins that join blood,
forms that emerge
little by little,
among songs and pathways,
necklace of flowers

worn by a goddess
throbbing in so deep
      a distance.

SEÑORA

A Martha Carpio

En algún lugar de los latidos
se agazapa

                    rugido y aleteo,
fulgor de luna

                entre las lianas

Concentrada tras la piel
su amargura antigua
respira entre burbujas

Alta entre montañas,
hermosa de imperio implacable,
tibia

        tiniebla.

LADY

For Martha Carpio

Somewhere among heartbeats
she crouches
                bellowing and flapping her wings,
the moon's brightness
                appearing through vines

Concentrated beneath her skin
an old bitterness
breathes between bubbles

Tall among mountains,
beautiful and of implacable bearing,
warm
        shadow.

MANDALA INFINITO

A Samuel López

Basta un instante,
un soplo bendecido
para llegar al fondo,
al sitio donde la materia se suspende
absorta en sí misma
para diluirse en el todo,
sin identidad ni apegos,
sin temor

Ahí nace todo fuego,
confines del tiempo,
ramillete de orígenes iluminados

Ahí nace el movimiento,
placas tectónicas
que sostienen todo núcleo,
toda periferia

Ahí nace el amor
y nacen también
el dolor y el canto

Y la voluntad del latido,
el vuelo iridiscente del aliento,
es un ave que al fin se encuentra
libre para reconocer su origen

Libre para recordar
la potestad del Ser
y la luminiscencia de la carne

Libre para entregarse a la caída
de lo grande en lo pequeño,
a la heredad de los milagros
de los que somos parte

INFINITE MANDALA

For Samuel López

One instant is enough,
one sanctified breath
to reach the depth,
that place where all matter is suspended
absorbed in itself
dissolving in everything,
without identity or attachments,
without fear

All fire is born there,
the limits of time,
a bouquet of illuminated beginnings

All movement is born there,
tectonic plates
sustaining every nucleus,
every periphery

All love is born there
and also
pain and song

And the heartbeat's will,
breath's iridescent flight,
a bird that is finally free
to recognize its origin

Free to remember
the power of Being
and luminescence of flesh

Free to give itself to the descent
of the immensity in what is small,
free to inherit the miracles
to which we belong

Libre para aceptar
el mandato del deleite
sembrado en cada germen
que se descubre vida

Porque todo permanece ahí,
un paso más allá
de cada cuerpo,
un grano de arena más allá
de lo evidente,
recordando la grandeza en
un himno interminable

Todo pulsa ahí,
más allá de la penumbra y la agonía
donde el dolor no es sufrimiento
y el amor no conoce el miedo

Todo pulsa ahí y es belleza,
todo pulsa ahí y es perfecto,
todo pulsa ahí
y es un mandala infinito
en cada cuerpo.

Free to accept
the mandate of delight
sown in every seed
that finds life

Because it all remains there,
one step beyond
each body,
one grain of sand beyond
that which is evident,
remembering the greatness
in an endless hymn

Everything pulses there,
beyond gloom and agony
where pain is no longer suffering
and love knows no fear

Everything pulses there and is beauty,
everything pulses there and is perfect,
everything pulses there
and is an infinite mandala
in every being.

EN VUELO

A Lupita Castro

Me sumergí en los confines de la belleza,
en el sitio donde nace el río
claro y profundo de la vida

En fractales todo cambió de configuración
y se abrieron mundos desconocidos,
brillantes himnos,
      tambores hondos,
        luciérnagas de fuego

Todo está ahí
y yo no lo veía
hasta que me quité
para que existiera

Y entonces ocurrió el milagro:
me salieron alas,
         el salmón alcanzó las cimas
tras todas las tormentas

Al fin la oruga vio la luz
y se asombró de tanta suculencia,
y la mariposa bailó con el pulso
de la tierra,
describiendo dibujos encendidos
de brillo incalculable.

IN FLIGHT

For Lupita Castro

I submerged myself within beauty's boundaries,
in the place where the river of life
emerges clear and deep

In fractals everything changes shape
and unknown worlds appear,
brilliant hymns,
       profound drums,
       fireflies made of fire

It is all there
and I did not see it
until I removed myself
so it could exist

And then the miracle occurred:
I sprouted wings,
             salmon made it upstream
against all obstacle

Larva finally saw the light
startled by so much succulence,
and the butterfly danced
with earth's pulse,
describing brilliant drawings
of incalculable light.

DANZA

A Andrea Losada

Una llamarada ondulante
levanta los huesos,
urna del corazón
para acercarlo al cielo

Espigas se abren en las manos
y los pies danzan
sobre el amor,
alrededor de él,
        tesoro inaudito

Todo surge en alabanza
hasta alcanzar los cálidos filamentos
        de lo infinito.

DANCE

For Andrea Losada

An undulating flash
raises bones,
bringing the heart's urn
closer to the sky

Sprigs bloom in hands
and feet dance
on love,
and around it,
          astonishing treasure

All arises in praise
until reaching the warm filaments
          of the infinite.

ETÉREA

Se desdobla en el sueño,
          Anaconda
que todo lo abraza,
se aparece en el camino
y habla en otros ojos

Anoche llegó ataviada
con un ropaje de cielo,
mucho menos amarga,
          etérea

Vine a pedirle ayuda
para liberar el capullo
que me resquebrajó,
colgando entre jirones

La urdimbre dulce
del palo santo
dibujó renglones interminables

El dolor que provocó
su estilete
no cimbró mi cuerpo,
ni me llevó a la agonía
de la mente

Las cuerdas tensadas
eran de mi pecho,
limón goteando lágrimas,
hasta que me volteó
desde el fondo
sin violencia
y me hizo sacudir
los sedimentos del dolor

Se puede vomitar llanto
          —no lo sabía—
dolor incrustado en el fondo del corazón,
recipiente turbio

ETHEREAL.

In my dream she uncoiled,
       Anaconda
who embraces all,
she appears upon the path
speaking in other eyes

Last night she arrived dressed
in a suit of sky,
much less bitter,
       ethereal

I came to ask her help
I wanted to free myself
from the cocoon that contained me,
still hanging in strips

The sweet warp
of *palo santo*
painted interminable lines

The pain its stiletto
produced
didn't do my body in,
nor bring me to agony
of mind

The tensed ropes
were from my breast,
tears dripping from a lime,
until she turned
without violence
from the depths
and helped me shake off
my sediments of pain

One can vomit sobs
       —I didn't know—
pain embedded in the heart's floor,
murky receptacle

Como un guante
me volteó hacia sí
        Cielo,
me limpió los ojos
con el ámbar de una vela
y desprendió mis costras
ya marchitas,
gramos que pesaban toneladas

Y el aliento entonces
encontró otros caminos
para traer el viento,
para abrirse a un mundo
despojado ya
de todos los vestigios.

Like a glove
she turned toward me
            Sky ,
wiped my eyes
with a candle's amber
and removed my scabs
shriveled now,
ounces that weighed tons

Then breath discovered
other ways
of delivering wind,
of opening to a world
already divested
of every residue.

EPíloGo

EPILOGUE

LA SOGA DE LOS MUERTOS

I

Vengo de entre muertos
que caminan
con pies vendados de amnesia,
transitando vidas
de concreto interminable

Muertos que no se encuentran
porque ya se fueron,
o quizá nunca llegaron,
atrapados en una urbe
de espejismos

Pero entre esos muertos la he visto,
con un fulgor de formas incandescentes
y la geométrica estructura de la vida
        más allá de la tempestad

La he sentido abrasándome por dentro,
        fuego que se extiende
con la sencillez de lo imprescindible

Con sabiduría perfecta
dio vida a mi muerte,
para huir de una dentellada sin sentido

Me hizo refulgir desde lo más hondo
curando mi gangrena,
respirando sobre mi asfixia,
devolviendo miembros amputados

Me ha levantado de la fosa común
donde yacen todos los miedos
aferrados a una noche descompuesta

        Me contó los secretitos
        de la tierra y del agua

THE ROPE OF THE DEAD

I

I come from among the dead
who walk
their feet bound by amnesia,
traveling lives
of endless concrete

Dead who cannot find themselves
because they're already gone,
or perhaps haven't yet arrived,
trapped in a metropolis
of mirages

But among those dead I have seen her,
with the brilliance of incandescence
and geometrical structure of life
           beyond the storm

I have felt her embracing me from within,
           a fire that spreads
with the simplicity of that which is needed

With perfect wisdom
she gave life to my death,
to escape needless greed

She made me shine in the depths
cured my gangrene,
breathed life into my suffocation,
returned amputated limbs

She raised me from the common grave
where all fears reside
clinging to unsettled night

           *She told me the little secrets
           of earth and of water*

Me contó los secretitos
del fuego y de los vientos

Transfusión de vida
que se esparce en sudor
electrizante,
la soga de los muertos
me ha despojado de todo,
como a un diamante
que estuviera cubierto de carbón
y en el olvido.

II

Un capullo se disolvió desde su núcleo

Sachamama Amoru,
      gran Serpiente
            despojada de pieles,
renaciendo,
una noche eclipsó mis atavismos,
y quedé desnuda
      de mí
conmigo

El camino se llenó
de flores incendiadas,
de aguas pulcras
sumadas a mi boca,
picos blancos
      altos como un suspiro,
lunas cruzadas
de lianas bendecidas
en la selva,
rostros nuevos
como orquídeas desconocidas,
luces que gravitan
a mi paso
con el pulso de guardianes,
y el ritmo de icaros
      y silencios.

She told me the little secrets
of the fire and the winds

Transfusion of life
scattering
in electrifying sweat,
the rope of the dead
has dispossessed me of everything,
like a diamond
forgotten
and covered in coal.

II

My cocoon dissolves from its nucleus out

Sachamama Amoru,
            great Serpent
                        dispossessed of skins,
being delivered again,
a single night eclipsed old habits,
and I was naked
            alone
with myself

The path filled
with brilliant flowers,
pure water
for my mouth,
white peaks
            tall as a sigh,
moons crossed
by sacred vines
in the jungle,
new faces
like undiscovered orchids,
lights rotating
as I pass
with the pulse of guardians,
the rhythm of the chants
            and silences.

III

Un largo camino he andado
hasta llegar a ella,
en la oscuridad
he percibido su latido,
tras caídas y tropiezos,
cicatrices que ya son humo

El camino me encontró a mí
y me dio a elegir
entre vivir con un trozo de mi cuerpo
    —de mi vida—
a rastras
o comenzar desde un principio
y sin reservas

Porque dando tumbos había tocado,
dando tumbos, rasguñando,
había mirado,
dando tumbos y sin paladear
había comido

Un amor desconocido
pulsa en las orillas,
reverencia honda,
frente que toca la tierra,
labios que besan la distancia

Neonata perlada de líquido amniótico,
luciérnaga que descubrió su luz
    y su alimento

Hoy amaneció.

III

I have walked long distances
to get to her,
in the darkness
I have felt her heartbeat,
tripping and falling,
scabs that are smoke now

The road found me
and let me choose
between living with a piece of my body
          —of my life—
dragging behind
or starting afresh
and without reserve

Because stumbling I had touched,
stumbling, clawing,
I had seen,
stumbling and without tasting
I had eaten

An unknown love
beat along the shores,
a deep reverence,
forehead pressed to earth,
lips kissing the distance

Pearly newborn of amniotic liquid,
firefly who discovered her light
          and sustenance

Dawned today.

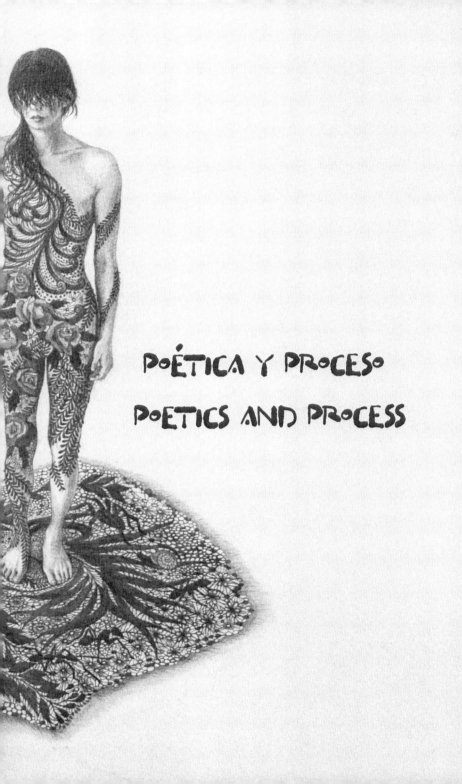

POÉTICA Y PROCESO

POETICS AND PROCESS

A CONVERSATION WITH MARÍA VÁZQUEZ VALDEZ

The Operating System: María, would you speak to us about your creative process in general? Do you write every day? A little? A lot?

María: Yes, I write every day, as part of a creative practice that isn't limited to poetry; I also write essays, reviews, and academic texts on cultural and editorial subjects. I don't know if I write a little poetry or a lot, but I almost always feel it isn't enough because I'd love to have the time to write a great deal more, especially poetry. I don't have a set writing schedule, and the quality as well as the quantity of my poetry depends on the moment. I'd say my poetry flows much more easily when I'm traveling, far from the usual everyday demands.

TOS: Why do you think you are a poet?

María: I believe I'm a poet because poetry, for me, is the clearest, most profound and most beautiful point of entrance I know through which to experience myself in relation to my world and within myself. It is in poetry that I find the greatest possibility of transforming experience, of putting it into words, of transmitting it in a multiplicity of universes... and also of articulating or sharing it with others. It is how I communicate best. I don't believe I am a poet out of necessity, but rather out of drive and desire. It is in poetry that I find the space where I can live with most freedom and yearning.

TOS: When did you first think of yourself as a poet? And do you feel entirely comfortable calling yourself that, or are there other identities you prefer?

María: I actually assumed my identity as a poet at a very young age. My father taught me to read before I was three, and from that moment on I fell completely and definitively in love with words. I discovered their beauty on the page and in their sounds, in their pronunciation and meaning. At five I began reading poetry, and before I was ten I was writing it. From then on, I considered myself a poet; although I do use other titles professionally: editor, journalist, writer or photographer.

TOS: How would you describe the cultural and social role you play within your literary/artistic community, and beyond?

María: I have been a part of my artistic and literary community from the time I was very young, first in Mexico and then in other countries as well: writing poetry, doing arts journalism, interviewing other writers and artists, writing chronicles and so forth. I've also edited a number of book and magazine collections for publishing projects, mostly having to do with poetry. This is about vocation, but also because I know how much there is to be done--not only in Mexico but throughout the world--in terms of disseminating culture and art (and poetry in particular) in places where political manipulation and mass media overwhelm us with a consumerist mentality to the detriment of authentic artistic expression. There's a lot to be done to promote meaningful art, to cultivate artistic expressions that counteract the imposition of society's commodity values, its promotion of superficial and frivolous products, products that push individual expression to the margins. There's so much to be done in the realm of poetry alone, in the search for an expression that transcends stereotypes, the senseless repetition of that which sells and promotes interests that are contrary to the authentic voice. There is a lot to be done in terms of questioning establishment values and politically and culturally established forms, the fictitious borders that divide us, the absurd roles that define us and the unjust prejudices that shape our identities, identities vital to our survival. And we have a lot to do, as well, when it comes to listening, to sharing and promoting the voices of those who are least often heard in mainstream communication, but who have a deep and vital message for all our societies today.

For all of this, the cultural and social roles we play demand that we disseminate poetry by every means possible, by which I mean writing it, publishing it, translating it, reviewing it and more. For me, this means sharing my poetry in different venues and ways, including importantly through my body, my experience and my word.

TOS: Can you talk about your creative process, María, when and how you transform individual poems into a single coherent body or book? For example, with Kawsay *did you visualize the poems as a series from the beginning, or realize you were writing a book as the process progressed? Did you intend to write a book of poems before your experience in the jungle?*

María: *Kawsay, The Flame of the Jungle* is the third book of poems I've published and the fifth I've written. Prior to it were *Caldero* (1999) and *Estancias* (2004), as well as seven other books in various genres (interview collections, essays, art books, and books for children and adolescents). My first two poetry books developed slowly, and writing them was a very different experience from the one I had with *Kawsay*.

My intention in going to the Amazon jungle of Peru wasn't specifically to write a book, but to give myself to the experience itself, one that was intensely unique and unusual for me. Those days of absolute silence, almost total fasting, cleansing the organism with plants considered sacred by the community, without electricity or running water, without the devices we generally have in our lives, without the presence of other people, and devoid of ordinary consumer products (such as soap, toothpaste, lotions and so forth), were a revelation to me. They didn't only place in stark contrast the world I knew, but revealed me to myself. The book didn't take shape slowly. It exploded as a torrent I was unable to hold back, nor did I want to. It sprang forth in a way I hadn't known before. And the poems appeared almost in the order they do in the book. A few--the very last ones--were finished after I got home. They became the epilogue, but I'd also written them with the same abandon. I even wrote some in the street, as I was walking, because the impetus continued for a while. Of course, not everything that I wrote is in the book. What appears in *Kawsay* represents a selection and refinement of the material I'd accumulated. And I see it as a part of the personal purification the experience in the jungle produced in me.

TOS: María, are there any formal structures or other literary "rules" that you favor when you write? Have you had important poetry mentors? Any particular readings or physical places that have influenced your work? And if so, how?

María: No particular literary structures or "rules." The poem itself dictates its rhythm and intrinsic structure, the number of syllables and rhyme (if any). In the past, there were times when I did play with a range of metrics and literary formulae, as a way of experimenting and also to help me understand certain currents and styles.

As far as influences go, I think reading poetry and knowing poets are always influential. Along the way a certain depuration takes place. As one learns more, one's poetic identity is shaped. In my case, for example, a great deal of my poetic education can be traced to my participation in *Alforja*, a poetry journal founded by José Vicente Anaya and that we published in Mexico for more than a decade (1997-2008). During that time, we produced 45 quarterly monographic issues of more than 150 pages each. This put me in touch with a huge number of poets from many different countries, and I'm sure the experience resonated in my own poetry as well as in my preferences as a reader.

In my work as an editor I have also found important mentors from time to time. Right now, for example, I am editing a collection of Sor Juana

Inés de la Cruz's poetry, and this has made it possible for me to study her work in a very profound way. Translating has also brought me mentors. One of them, without doubt, is Margaret Randall, who is a master of poetry, life, and the positions she takes with regard to art, politics, gender, and consciousness. I was fortunate to interview Margaret in 2002 for *Voces desdobladas / Unfolded Voices*, an anthology of women poets from Mexico and the United States that appeared bilingually in 2004. Since then I have been translating her poetry (four published books to date), and she has been an important influence. I have been influenced, as well, by the other poets in that anthology: Elsa Cross, Isabel Fraire, Mónica Mansour, Sharon Olds, and Anne Waldman.

Still, I will say that although I have read a great deal of diverse poetry, some of it from distant cultures, I believe the challenge is always to develop an authentic voice of one's own, a voice that works beyond any sort of influence. And, of course, many countries and cultures with which I've had the privilege of having contact have also been decisive, not only in my poetry but also in my life. A great deal of my poetry has been written out of the profound astonishment I've felt for certain places on this planet, its people and history. More than a determining influence, these places have inspired me.

TOS: Finally, María, how was the Mexican edition of Kawsay *received? What has this book represented for you?*

María: After finishing the book in 2011, *Kawsay* waited several years for publication. It finally came out at the end of 2016 and beginning of 2017, and immediately made an impact. It was featured in the media before I launched it at the 2017 Zacatecas Book Fair, and then at the Casa del Poeta in Mexico City in August of that year. At both events, I was surprised by its reception, among the other presenters as well as the public. The experience in the Amazon jungle found a voice in my poetry that was able to go beyond what I had written to that point. And I really think that was the original intention: that this poetry transcend me as an author just as the experience itself transcended me as a human being. Through these poems I have been able to communicate something I discovered and brought from the jungle, not just for myself but for others.

Kawsay also marks a new moment in my writing, a kind of parting of the waters so to speak, a very different experience from those I've had up to now. It is a poetry that surges as if from the mouth of a volcano, one that I am unable to hold back. It is also the testimony of a fundamental experience in my life, an encounter, a rebirth of my poetic voice as well as of my cosmic vision, a new opportunity that reminds me that the possibility of dawn exists even in the darkest nights; because this is how the experience took root in my own life: I was feeling hopeless, in a very dark place, and found a thread of light in the jungle.

Kawsay also has its roots in my recognition of, and deep gratitude to, ancestral cultures, represented in this case by the Shipibo Indians and their plants and primal wisdom. It's a tribute to ancient ways of knowledge, nature in its naked and most exquisite exuberance, and to the privileged connection we humans have with it. *Kawsay* is gratitude to that flame of the jungle that burns within and beyond all that is human in order to imbue life with that which is most profound. A jungle flame that is also meant to pay tribute to the first book I ever read, at the age of five: *Call of the Wild* by Jack London. From that moment, perhaps without being totally aware of it, I felt called to that place that so many years later I would have the privilege of assimilating with all my senses. *Kawsay* is a praise song to that flame that is alive and burns there, a flame that is also a call, inviting us to reignite the bit of ash that is always waiting to become fire again.

María Vázquez Valdez. *Photo by the author.*

ABOUT THE AUTHOR

MARÍA VÁZQUEZ VALDEZ nació en Zacatecas, México. Es poeta, editora, traductora y fotógrafa. Autora de los poemarios *Caldero* (1999), *Estancias* (2004), y *Kawsay. La llama de la selva* (2017); del libro de ensayos *Estaciones del albatros* (2008); del libro bilingüe de entrevistas *Voces desdobladas / Unfolding Voices* (2004); y de cinco libros para niños y jóvenes. Ha traducido varios libros. María estudió la licenciatura en periodismo, la maestría en edición, y actualmente concluye el doctorado en teoría crítica. Formó parte del consejo editorial de la revista *Alforja* desde su fundación, y actualmente colabora con el equipo editorial de la Academia Mexicana de la Lengua y con diversos proyectos académicos y culturales. Ha sido jefa de publicaciones de la Unión de Universidades de América Latina (UDUAL), directora editorial de la revista *Arcilla Roja*, editora en la revista GPMX de Greenpeace y en Editorial Santillana. Ha recibido becas y apoyos del Fondo Nacional para la Cultura y las Artes, la Secretaría de Cultura y el Fideicomiso para la Cultura México-Estados Unidos. *Kawsay. La Llama de la selva* tiene sus raíces en una experiencia con los indios Shipibo de la selva amazónica de Perú.

MARÍA VÁZQUEZ VALDEZ was born in Zacatecas, Mexico. She is a poet, editor, translator and photographer. Her books include the poetry collections *Caldero* (1999), *Estancias* (2004), and *Kawsay. La llama de la selva* (2017); the book of essays *Estaciones del albatros* (2008); the bilingual book of interviews *Voces desdobladas / Unfolding Voices* (2004); and five books for children and young readers. She has translated several books of poetry. María received a degree in journalism, a Masters in editing, and is currently finishing a Doctorate in critical theory. She was part of the editorial board of *Alforja* from its foundation, and is now a member of the Mexican Academy of the Language's editorial team, as well as of other academic and cultural projects. She has been the director of publications at the Union of Latin American Universities (UDUAL), editor in chief of the literary magazine *Arcilla Roja*, editor of Greenpeace's GPMX magazine, and editor at Editorial Santillana. She has received grants and support from Mexican government institutions. The poems in *Kawsay. La Llama de la selva* have their roots in an experience with the Shipibo Indians of Peru's Amazon jungle.

https://mariavazquezvaldez.jimdo.com/
maresdecierto@gmail.com

Margaret Randall. *Photo: Chris Felver*

TRANSLATION BY

MARGARET RANDALL (New York 1936), poeta, traductora, fotógrafa y activista social, ha publicado más de 100 libros, entre ellos los de su propia poesía y prosa y traducciones de la obra de otros. En 2017 recibió la Medalla del Mérito Literario de Literatura en el Bravo, Ciudad Juárez, México.

MARGARET RANDALL (New York 1936), poet, translator, photographer and social activist, has published more than 100 books, including her own poetry and prose and translations. In 2017, she received the Medal of Literary Merit from Literatura en el Bravo, Ciudad Juárez, Mexico.

www.margaretrandall.org

TRANSLATOR'S NOTE

Kawsay is a collection of poems, but it is also an experience, told in the voice of the poet as she moves from questions to answers, from beginning to an end which is not an end but an opening to further questions, which is to say, to life in the deeper sense. María Vázquez entrusted herself to a shaman of the Shipibo community in the Amazon jungle of Peru, lived in isolation for a prescribed number of days, ate and drank only what her fast permitted, exited her body and entered the collective body beyond that which ordinarily limits our senses, and left behind the constrictions to which modernity ties us. This is not the superficial "new age" adventure of someone momentarily embracing whatever esoteric fad comes along, but the profound engagement of a woman who has traveled the world and is familiar with the ritualistic practices of diverse cultures. Because she is a poet, she was able to transform this experience into words, into the journey of poems contained in the book you hold in your hands. Chizuko Osato's drawings emerge on the page with similar authenticity and power; Chizuko herself underwent the same experience in the same place exactly one year later; they complete the magic of this offering.

Although I have never gone through such an experience, I know María and her poetry. We have worked together for years, sharing poems, translating one another's work, editing anthologies and giving readings together--in Mexico as well as the United States. After she translated my collection, *Into Another Time: Grand Canyon Reflections*, we traveled together to Grand Canyon, sharing the wonder of a landscape that transcends time. I read *Kawsay* and found myself rendering the poems into English before even consulting with the poet. As I translated, María's words drew me into another world where time is also transcended, consciousness changed. By coincidence (or not), when I read this book I had also just translated a memoir by the Peruvian anthropologist Stefano Varese, in which he writes of similar initiation ceremonies among the Shipibo. As a poet, María had approached the same shift through a different genre.

These are extremely challenging times. The rise of neo-fascism in our country and in other parts of the world demands we draw upon multiple pathways of resistance and learn to weave them into coherent material for struggle. The old modes have shown themselves to be partial, narrow, incapable by themselves of bringing about definitive change. We have been able to make progress in some areas—Black and other youth of color organizing successfully, women joining forces to topple those committing sexual harassment and abuse, a new sanctuary movement defending vulnerable immigrants, state and city governments stepping up to make the commitments and fight the battle to combat climate change that has been abandoned by the federal government—but we have yet to develop an overall strategy that will permit us to wage the life and death struggle successfully. To this end we need every means at our disposal: political, social, cultural, artistic, psychological, spiritual, and of the imagination. Many poets and visual artists, singer/songwriters and theater people, translators and independent publishers are harnessing our creativity to this end.

Current Washington policy aims to erect walls: between this country and our neighbors; between citizens of different classes, races, and genders; between the language of Armaggedon and that of the magical realism in which we all live. In these poems, María Vázquez breaks down the wall between our coopted lives and the mindfulness to which we all have access through experiences such as the one she references here.

This bilingual edition of *Kawsay*, published by The Operating System, is a perfect marriage of ancient ritual with a press that conceives of its books as community tools. I am proud to have been part of this effort by María Vázquez Valdez, Chizuko Osato, and Lynne DeSilva-Johnson to make this book—that enjoyed great success in Mexico--available to an English readership.

Margaret Randall
Winter, 2017.

ILLUSTRATIONS BY

CHIZUKO OSATO nació en Japón. Estudió Bellas Artes y Música en la Universidad de Tokio. Ha recibido premios en la Bienal de Valencia, España, y el Fonart en Monterrey, México. De 1995 a 2014 vivió en México, y esta obra gráfica suya fue realizada durante una estancia en la selva amazónica peruana.

CHIZUKO OSATO was born in Japan. She studied fine arts and music at the University of Tokio. Her work has received prizes at the Biennale in Valencia, Spain, and from Fonart in Monterrey, Mexico. From 1995 to 2014 she lived in Mexico, and the drawings that illustrate this book were made during a stay in the Amazon jungle of Peru.

GLOSSARIUM:
UNSILENCED TEXTS AND MODERN TRANSLATIONS

The Operating System's *Glossarium: Unsilenced Texts* series was established in early 2016 in an effort to recover silenced voices outside and beyond the familiar poetic canon, seeking out and publishing both contemporary translations and little or unknown out of print texts, in particular those under siege by restrictive regimes and silencing practices in their home (or adoptive) countries.

The term "Glossarium" derives from latin/greek and is defined as "a collection of glosses or explanations of words, especially of words not in general use, as those of a dialect, locality or an art or science, or of particular words used by an old or a foreign author." The series was initiated by and is curated by OS Founder and Managing Editor Lynne DeSilva-Johnson, with the help of a wide range of global allies, collaborators and friends.

Other active and forthcoming titles in this series include:

Ashraf Fayadh, *Instructions Within* (Arabic-English)
trans. Mona Kareem, Jonathan Wright, and Mona Zaki.
ed. Lynne DeSilva-Johnson, Ammiel Alcalay, Pierre Joris

Gregory Randall's award winning memoir of life in Cuba
To Have Been There Then (Estar Allí Entonces)
translated from the Spanish by Margaret Randall

Jerome Rothenberg and Harold Cohen, *Flower World Variations, Expanded Edition.* (original printing, 1984, Membrane Press)
Text derived / translated from the Yaqui Deer Dances.

Chely Lima, *Lo Que Les Dijo El Licántropo / What the Werewolf Told Them.* (Spanish-English/dual-language), trans. Margaret Randall

La Comandante Maya, Rita Valdivia. (Spanish-English/dual-language)
trans. Margaret Randall.

Israel Domínguez, *Viaje de Regreso / Return Trip,* (Spanish-English/dual-language) trans. Margaret Randall, with art by Jose Parla and JR.

Mehdi Navid, *The Book of Sounds* (Farsi-English/dual-language)
trans. Tina Rahimi, with art by Iman Raad

Marta Zelwan/Krystyna Sakowicz, *Śnienie / Dreaming*
(Polish-English/dual-language) trans. Victoria Miluch

Hélène Sanguinetti, *Alparegho, Pareil-À-Rien / Alparegho, Like Nothing Else* (French-English/dual-language), trans. Ann Cefola

Bijan Elahi, *High Tide Of The Eyes* (Farsi-English/dual-language)
trans. Rebecca Ruth Gould and Kayvan Tahmasebian

WHY PRINT/DOCUMENT?

The Operating System uses the language "print document" to differentiate from the book-object as part of our mission to distinguish the act of documentation-in-book-FORM from the act of publishing as a backwards-facing replication of the book's agentive *role* as it may have appeared the last several centuries of its history. Ultimately, I approach the book as TECHNOLOGY: one of a variety of printed documents (in this case, bound) that humans have invented and in turn used to archive and disseminate ideas, beliefs, stories, and other evidence of production.

Ownership and use of printing presses and access to (or restriction of printed materials) has long been a site of struggle, related in many ways to revolutionary activity and the fight for civil rights and free speech all over the world. While (in many countries) the contemporary quotidian landscape has indeed drastically shifted in its access to platforms for sharing information and in the widespread ability to "publish" digitally, even with extremely limited resources, the importance of publication on physical media has not diminished. In fact, this may be the most critical time in recent history for activist groups, artists, and others to insist upon learning, establishing, and encouraging personal and community documentation practices. Hear me out.

With The OS's print endeavors I wanted to open up a conversation about this: the ultimately radical, transgressive act of creating PRINT /DOCUMENTATION in the digital age. It's a question of the archive, and of history: who gets to tell the story, and what evidence of our life, our behaviors, our experiences are we leaving behind? We can know little to nothing about the future into which we're leaving an unprecedentedly digital document trail — but we can be assured that publications, government agencies, museums, schools, and other institutional powers that be will continue to leave BOTH a digital and print version of their production for the official record. Will we?

As a (rogue) anthropologist and long time academic, I can easily pull up many accounts about how lives, behaviors, experiences — how THE STORY of a time or place — was pieced together using the deep study of correspondence, notebooks, and other physical documents which are no longer the norm in many lives and practices. As we move our creative behaviors towards digital note taking, and even audio and video, what can we predict about future technology that is in any way assuring that our stories will be accurately told – or told at all? How will we leave these things for the record?

In these documents we say:
        WE WERE HERE, WE EXISTED, WE HAVE A DIFFERENT STORY

                                    - Lynne DeSilva-Johnson, Founder/Managing Editor,
                                    THE OPERATING SYSTEM, Brooklyn NY 2017

TITLES IN THE
PRINT / DOCUMENT COLLECTION

Śnienie / Dreaming - Marta Zelwan/Krystyna Sakowicz, (Polish-English/dual-language) trans. Victoria Miluch
Alparegho: Pareil-À-Rien / Alparegho, Like Nothing Else - Hélène Sanguinetti (French-English/dual-language), trans. Ann Cefola
High Tide Of The Eyes - Bijan Elahi (Farsi-English/dual-language) trans. Rebecca Ruth Gould and Kayvan Tahmasebian

An Absence So Great and Spontaneous It Is Evidence of Light - Anne Gorrick [2018]
The Book of Everyday Instruction - Chloe Bass [2018]
Executive Orders Vol. II - a collaboration with the Organism for Poetic Research [2018]
One More Revolution - Andrea Mazzariello [2018]
The Suitcase Tree - Filip Marinovich [2018]
Chlorosis - Michael Flatt and Derrick Mund [2018]
Sussuros a Mi Padre - Erick Sáenz [2018]
Sharing Plastic - Blake Nemec [2018]
The Book of Sounds - Mehdi Navid (Farsi dual language, trans. Tina Rahimi) [2018]
In Corpore Sano : Creative Practice and the Challenged Body [Anthology, 2018]; Lynne DeSilva-Johnson and Jay Besemer, co-editors
Abandoners - Lesley Ann Wheeler [2018]
Jazzercise is a Language - Gabriel Ojeda-Sague [2018]
Return Trip / Viaje Al Regreso - Israel Dominguez; (Spanish-English dual language) trans. Margaret Randall [2018]
Born Again - Ivy Johnson [2018]
Attendance - Rocío Carlos and Rachel McLeod Kaminer [2018]
Singing for Nothing - Wally Swist [2018]
The Ways of the Monster - Jay Besemer [2018]
Walking Away From Explosions in Slow Motion - Gregory Crosby [2018]
The Unspoken - Bob Holman [Bowery Books imprint - 2018]
Field Guide to Autobiography - Melissa Eleftherion [2018]
Kawsay: The Flame of the Jungle - María Vázquez Valdez (Spanish-English dual language) trans. Margaret Randall [2018]
CHAPBOOK SERIES 2018 : Greater Grave - Jacq Greyja; Needles of Itching Feathers - Jared Schlickling; Want-Catcher - Adra Raine; We, The Monstrous - Mark DuCharme

Lost City Hydrothermal Field - Peter Milne Greiner [2017]
An Exercise in Necromancy - Patrick Roche [Bowery Poetry Imprint, 2017]
Love, Robot - Margaret Rhee[2017]
La Comandante Maya - Rita Valdivia (dual language, trans. Margaret Randall) [2017]
The Furies - William Considine [2017]
Nothing Is Wasted - Shabnam Piryaei [2017]
Mary of the Seas - Joanna C. Valente [2017]
Secret-Telling Bones - Jessica Tyner Mehta [2017]

DOC U MENT
/däkyəmənt/

First meant "instruction" or "evidence," whether written or not.

noun - a piece of written, printed, or electronic matter that provides information or evidence or that serves as an official record
verb - record (something) in written, photographic, or other form
synonyms - paper - deed - record - writing - act - instrument

[*Middle English, precept, from Old French, from Latin documentum, example, proof, from docre, to teach; see dek- in Indo-European roots.*]

Who is responsible for the manufacture of value?

Based on what supercilious ontology have we landed in a space where we vie against other creative people in vain pursuit of the fleeting credibilities of the scarcity economy, rather than freely collaborating and sharing openly with each other in ecstatic celebration of MAKING?

While we understand and acknowledge the economic pressures and fear-mongering that threatens to dominate and crush the creative impulse, we also believe that ***now more than ever we have the tools to relinquish agency via cooperative means,*** fueled by the fires of the Open Source Movement.

Looking out across the invisible vistas of that rhizomatic parallel country we can begin to see our community beyond constraints, in the place where intention meets resilient, proactive, collaborative organization.

Here is a document born of that belief, sown purely of imagination and will.
When we document we assert.
We print to make real, to reify our being there.
When we do so with mindful intention to address our process,
to open our work to others, to create beauty in words in space,
to respect and acknowledge the strength of the page we now hold physical,
a thing in our hand… we remind ourselves that, like Dorothy:
we had the power all along, my dears.

THE PRINT! DOCUMENT SERIES
is a project of
the trouble with bartleby
in collaboration with
the operating system